IGNITING TEACHER LEADERSHIP

How do I empower my teachers to lead and learn?

William
STERRETT

 Alexandria, VA USA

Website: www.ascd.org
E-mail: books@ascd.org

www.ascdarias.org

PAPERBACK ISBN: 978-1-4166-2177-5   ASCD product #SF116039

Also available as an e-book (see Books in Print for the ISBNs).

Library of Congress Cataloging-in-Publication Data

Names: Sterrett, William, author.
Title: Igniting teacher leadership : how do I empower my teachers to lead and learn? / William Sterrett.
Description: Alexandria, Virginia : ASCD, [2015] | Includes bibliographical references.
Identifiers: LCCN 2015038061 | ISBN 9781416621775 (pbk.)
Subjects: LCSH: Teacher-principal relationships--United States. | Professional learning communities--United States. | School improvement programs--United States.
Classification: LCC LB2832.2 .S84 2015 | DDC 371.1/06--dc23 LC record available at http://lccn.loc.gov/2015038061

23 22 21 20 19 18 17 16   1 2 3 4 5 6 7 8 9 10

IGNITING TEACHER LEADERSHIP

How do I empower my teachers to lead and learn?

Want to earn a free ASCD Arias e-book?
Your opinion counts! Please take 2–3 minutes to give
us your feedback on this publication. All survey
respondents will be entered into a drawing to
win an ASCD Arias e-book.

Please visit
www.ascd.org/ariasfeedback

Thank you!

Igniting Teacher Leadership

The principal pulled her office door shut and glanced around the empty administrative office lit only by a sliver of fading sunlight. She paused in front of the teachers' mailboxes, where 82 names were labeled beside their respective trays. She thought about the teachers who would be here first thing in the morning to collect their mail, notes, and memos, and she thought about the hundreds of students who were represented by those teachers—all of whom had thoughts, goals, challenges, and successes. Thoughts such as these:

- "I've enjoyed having a student teacher this semester. I can distinctly remember those challenges and successes when I was immersed into learning how to become a better teacher."
- "Wow, I'd love to stop by your classroom to see how you get these results . . . if I can just find the time."
- "How are you able to get Scottie to engage in class? I've been trying, but I sure could use any tips you can spare."
- "Where does she find the time to incorporate those new strategies? I'd love to learn more."

These statements and questions are examples that reveal our student-centered perspective as educators. We want the very best for *all* of our students. We prepare for years to become a teacher, we work tirelessly to engage and challenge our students, and we continually strive to meet the needs of today's learners. As educators, many of us have leadership roles or aspirations. We push ourselves to learn, grow, and innovate because we realize that leadership is continuously in flux. Nevertheless, when it comes to leadership, we must focus on growing one very important resource within the school: the teachers.

Jack Welch points out that leadership is not just about you. He observes, "Before you are a leader, success is all about growing yourself. When you become a leader, success is all about growing others" (2005, p. 61). It's important to emphasize growing others since we must, as leaders, focus on the shared, collaborative nature of school leadership. Regardless of your school's size, level, or location, the bottom line is that each leadership role depends on us moving forward and growing together to accomplish the goals of the entire school.

Research shows that school leadership is vital to an engaged school community and increased student achievement. One six-year study of more than 7,000 principals noted that "schools with high achievement were less likely to have a new principal and more likely to have had the same leader for several years" (Branch, Hanushek, & Rivkin, 2013, p. 68). Why is the principal so important? Simple: central to the role is the critical function of coordination in which the principal fosters, develops, and propels the collective effort of teaching and learning.

A recent Gallup study that was focused on the importance of school leadership found that "the principal's position aids coordination of separate contributors that collectively drive student achievement" (Gordon, 2013, p. 3). For far too long, many of these "separate contributors" have been hard-working teachers who have felt isolated and burnt out or who have been going through the motions of teaching without seeing substantial results in terms of learning. In that in-depth study of more than 90 principals and 4,500 teachers, "highly talented" principals demonstrated excellence in the following seven key areas (Gordon, 2013):

- **Goals and Expectations:** They present a vision for the school.
- **Teacher Support:** They work hard and are available for teachers.
- **Teacher Growth:** They are in classrooms often and help teachers use their individual strengths.
- **Student Focus:** They like students and do what is best for them.
- **Recognition of Success:** They celebrate and encourage teachers and success.
- **Positive Outlook:** They are optimistic and see problems as opportunities.
- **Parent Engagement:** They involve parents and inspire them to support the teachers.

We must support our teachers. It is the teacher who does the real work of instruction in the classroom. It is the teacher who usually greets each student into the learning community on Monday morning, even when it's hard. It is the teacher who must stay relevant—even decades after student teaching—for each incoming class. It is the teacher who is on the front line and must reassure anxious or worried parents. It is the teacher who must grow, innovate, and contribute to the profession.

As you can see, we ask much of our teachers, and unfortunately, we are losing too many of them—every year—because they feel burnt out, underappreciated, and overworked. As principal, we can have a huge effect in affirming teachers' sense of worth, strengthening a culture of collaboration, encouraging schoolwide innovation, and growing others professionally.

I am a firm believer that the role of the principal is uniquely positioned to deliver results, both in the short term and over many years. A principal can realize success through empowering his or her teachers (Sterrett, 2015). I frequently remind aspiring administrators that many of the best principals are collaborative leaders who see themselves as teachers; they think like teachers, listen like teachers, collaborate like teachers, and lead like teachers. And once they assume the principalship, they realize they are not the only teacher—or leader—in the building; they realize they must actively grow others in order to move the school forward in a significant manner.

This book will build on the leadership foundation established in my previous work—*Insights into Action* (Sterrett, 2011) and *Short on Time* (Sterrett, 2013). Here, we will zero in on the importance of nurturing and supporting the most vital resource in any educational setting—its people. We will examine ways to strengthen and affirm the work of teachers within our schools by examining our own habits as principals, and we will consider ways to focus on growing others rather than merely trying to lead alone.

As the saying goes, there is so much to do yet so little time. There is no excuse for school leaders, with increasing accountability and decreasing resources, not to empower the most valuable potential within their schools. It's time that leaders realize even greater success by igniting teacher leadership.

The Importance of Habit

As principal, my morning habits were fairly predictable. I would listen to upbeat music on the way to work while sipping my second cup of coffee. As I arrived, I parked close to the side entrance in an unmarked parking spot. (I was never a fan of the "principal's parking" designation common at many schools. My view was if an "early riser" beat me to the prime parking spot, he or she definitely deserved it!) Entering the school, I greeted the custodians, teachers, and office staff who were already there, and I often did a quick walk-around to ensure that everything was in good shape. I turned on my computer, put my lunch in the fridge, and sorted through the mail and notes that arrived before logging on to my e-mail. To maximize my time, I read through and responded to most of the new e-mails before the first bus arrived. Once the buses started to arrive, I would greet students, check in with teachers, and lead the morning announcements. Another school day started.

I am a creature of habit. Most educators like predictability, and we often try to structure our days around it. According to the U.S. Department of Education, there are more than 100,000 principals in U.S. elementary, middle, and high schools (Bitterman, Goldring, & Gray, 2013), and I'm willing to bet that a good percentage of them have very similar morning habits.

Recently, Duhigg (2012) noted that there is powerful potential in creating new "habit loops," which can lead to drastically different outcomes in our lives. Emphasizing habit is not new thinking, though. Over a century ago, William James wrote, "When we look at living creatures from an outward point of view, one of the first things that strike us is that they are bundles of habits" (1890, p. 3). As a teacher and principal, my "bundles of habits" usually involved following through on what I perceived to be the day's plan in a manner that supported learning and organization while squelching the "unknown." However, once I realized the power to create new habits, I transformed my role as leader. As principal, I sought to develop new habits to bolster collaboration, support the school vision, and foster a positive outlook as follows:

1. Organize one schoolwide field trip per year. I sought to lead by example in connecting learning outside the school with curricular goals.

2. Coauthor or present with teachers at conferences. It is important to affirm the work of teachers by promoting the notion that they have a voice when it comes to action research.

3. Celebrate faculty success. I realized I could transform faculty meetings by starting off with teacher-led affirmations that I support and promote as principal.

4. Provide immediate reflective feedback in observations. A walkthrough observation without feedback is worthless; teachers deserve our insights, encouragement, and questions.

5. Make it clear to the school community that I love my job. From calling out a bingo game to wearing character outfits, we principals lead by example when it comes to having a healthy sense of humor.

Few would dispute that principals should develop and support teacher leadership. However, in examining decades of teacher leadership, York-Barr and Duke state, "there is evidence to suggest that principal support of teacher leadership is more readily espoused than enacted" (2004, p. 274). As we are teachers ourselves, we principals must be more proactive and vigilant as we foster habits to develop, strengthen, and sustain teacher leadership within our schools.

Supporting Teachers

As principals, we are familiar with the phrase lifelong learners. We prioritize teaching and learning; we lead by example, seeking out and sharing insights from articles or conferences; and we are engaged in our professional learning networks (PLN). It's important to remember, though, that we are also lifelong teachers. The best administrators see themselves as teachers. Effective principals and superintendents never forget what it's like to have a classroom full of activity. They appreciate the value of rolling up their sleeves, wearing comfortable shoes, and engaging with students. Therefore, when school leaders make decisions about resource allocation, school improvement, or student learning, it's important to remember that this work moves forward because of the quality of teachers in the classroom. Our teachers will notice if we work each day like we are one of them. Indeed, the power of the principal is best realized through the collaborative work of teachers.

Listen to Teachers

To understand what teachers are thinking, we must listen to them. Sounds obvious, right? As principal, I often used end-of-meeting exit slips to ask teachers what was and wasn't working and to recognize other areas in which I might help. By carefully reading over their written thoughts and addressing them, I gained their trust. Teachers are extremely busy, and they don't always have time to craft a thoughtful letter of concern to the principal. This is why the principal must intentionally carve out time to listen.

Budd Dingwall was an award-winning principal in two states, earning the coveted National Blue Ribbon Schools distinction in Ohio (twice!) and the National Distinguished Principal award while serving in North Carolina. Budd's school, Codington Elementary School (CES), like all North Carolina public schools, participated in the North Carolina Teacher Working Conditions Survey, which is administered every two years. Budd's teachers clearly felt valued, particularly when compared with teachers across the state. The results are telling (North Carolina's Teacher Working Conditions Initiative, 2012):

- Teachers are recognized as educational experts. (100% at CES versus 83% statewide)
- Teachers are effective leaders in this school. (100% versus 88% statewide)
- The school leadership consistently supports teachers. (95% versus 79% statewide)
- Teachers feel comfortable raising issues and concerns that are important to them. (87% versus 71% statewide)
- The faculty are recognized for accomplishments. (93% versus 84% statewide)

When I asked Budd why his school was so different from other schools in the state in terms of what teachers thought, he offered a two-word response: "I listened." Budd made it a habit to host quarterly meetings with each teacher. He used a consistent, simple structure to guide those meetings; he would center the relatively brief meetings (no longer than 40 minutes) on the following two questions:

1. Please tell me how your students are doing.
2. What can I do to support you?

The first question allowed teachers to share successes and concerns, particularly those that went beyond the typical professional learning community (PLC) discussion. The second question allowed for a "direct line" to the principal that is unfortunately rare in today's busy school environment. Budd also empowered his assistant principal to lead these meetings (a decision necessary to make this approach work in a larger school). By listening to his teachers, he was able to firm up ideas about professional development, better understand his teachers' challenges, recognize their gains, and share success stories. He listened, and his teachers took notice.

Busy principals, take note: the best way to demonstrate that you value teachers is by listening to them . . . often. From short classroom visits to brief conversations in the hallway, we can move the work of the school forward by strengthening our listening habits, especially when it involves the teachers with whom we serve.

Support the Notion of Teacher as Learner

Even though we are focused on students' learning, let's not neglect to prioritize our own growth—as true lifelong learners—in the process. Even the most veteran teacher nearing retirement has something to learn—and likely to share with colleagues. One way we can help ignite others is by supporting the notion that our actions are influenced by our thinking and perspective. Costa and Garmston observe, "A person's actions are influenced by internal forces rather than overt behaviors. Therefore, cognitive coaches focus on the thought processes, values, and beliefs that motivate, guide, influence, and give rise to the overt behaviors" (2002, p. 13). This is a powerful reminder to busy principals. How do we encourage self-reflection and growth when it comes to thought processes, values, and beliefs? What are the implications in terms of how we encourage growth, provide feedback, and share leadership?

Identify Teacher Leadership

The notion of "teacher leadership" is not brand new. Yet not every school benefits from an active, engaged presence of teacher leadership. Citing research, Nathan Bond notes that teacher leaders "possess an insider's knowledge of the local school conditions [by knowing] their colleagues, the curriculum, and the culture of the school" (2015, p. 57). As such, they are a vital resource for leading efforts such as professional development, and they absolutely have a stake in the school's success.

It's important to consider possible teacher leader roles. To that end, the Teacher Leader Model Standards form a framework of seven domains that describe the many dimensions of teacher leadership:

- Domain I: Fostering a Collaborative Culture to Support Educator Development and Student Learning

- Domain II: Accessing and Using Research to Improve Practice and Student Learning
- Domain III: Promoting Professional Learning for Continuous Improvement
- Domain IV: Facilitating Improvements in Instruction and Student Learning
- Domain V: Promoting the Use of Assessments and Data for School and District Improvement
- Domain VI: Improving Outreach and Collaboration with Families and Community
- Domain VII: Advocating for Student Learning and the Profession (Teacher Leadership Exploratory Consortium, 2011, p. 9)

Practically speaking, the role of teacher leader can take on many forms in the school. Some schools or districts are positioned to allow for stipends or release time for these positions. For others, it's simply added to an educator's plate as the role of the teacher continues to expand. Here are just a few examples of ways in which teachers can lead.

Grade-level team leaders and department chairs: These lead teachers serve as a point of contact for coordinating PLC meetings, organizing grade-level events (e.g., field trips), and serving as a liaison with administration in representing his or her colleagues. As Bond notes, "teacher leaders who work with administrators and colleagues to develop and implement PLCs foster positive working relationships with colleagues, focus on issues import to the teachers, and promote greater student learning" (2015, p. 67).

New teacher mentors: Some veteran teachers serve as full-time mentors for teachers who are new to the school or district, but they most often serve as mentors to novice teachers—helping them with grade- or subject-specific instructional planning on top of practical assistance. These mentors serve as "teachers of teachers [who] help beginning teachers transform their thinking and classroom practice" (Davis et al., 2015, p. 72).

Curriculum innovators: All teachers should be involved in continuously reflecting on, developing, and improving their curriculum. Regardless of subject—from orchestra to chemistry—innovations and changes in curricula allow for growth and development. Often, district or state mandates necessitate intense, collaborative work with a structured outcome.

Technology liaison: This teacher innovator works to equip staff with new and emerging tools, strategies, and approaches intended to help enhance teaching and learning. When supported, he or she can lead by example in terms of "healthy risk taking" and encourage teachers to bolster student engagement by honing new strategies.

Special education lead teachers: These collaborative leaders positively affect their schools "by working closely with general education teachers to meet students' varying academic needs" (Smith, 2015, p. 82). This work often includes organizing and facilitating meetings and myriad paperwork to ensure compliance and collaboration.

Instructional coach: The role of a coach can vary by school and district, yet there is great potential for collaboration and instructional growth. From helping analyze data to serving as a reflective partner in instruction, from discussing curriculum to sharing best practices in classroom transitions, coaches can provide strong support both inside the classroom and in PLCs across a school or district.

Arts lead teachers: Although "core" subjects are increasingly emphasized in the accountability era, there is great value in a teacher who can "witness and nurture a learner's creative side" through arts instruction (DeRosa & Trostle Brand, 2015, p. 93). Such teachers can also collaborate with their colleagues to infuse the arts across the curriculum. In fact, specialists who help deliver instruction in art, music, physical education/health, library/media, and many other so-called non-core areas often benefit from a schoolwide perspective and are adept at key leadership aspects, from scheduling to school improvement.

These are just a few examples of key roles that lead by innovating, connecting, and fostering collaboration. Some teachers may not have an additional title that reflects this role, yet they still put in the work required to sustain healthy learning spaces, strengthen collaboration, and meet the needs of individual students in powerful, meaningful ways. By striving to ignite and grow teacher leadership, the principal cannot take for granted these valuable roles. They must be developed and supported with care, caution, and gratitude. Here are a few key ways in which the principal can help grow and strengthen these roles:

Clarity and transparency: Having written, clearly understood role descriptions and a transparent process to determine how these roles are assumed are vitally important steps to ensuring success. The principal should ask, "Does the school community know what this role entails?"

Training and development: Often, successful veteran teachers are asked to assume roles with little training or ongoing professional development support. The principal should ask, "How can we fully equip this person for this role? What school and district resources are available to ensure that he or she continues to learn and grow while in this role?"

Incentives and affirmation: When possible, the school and district should recognize the vast amount of time and energy needed for these roles, particularly when they are "above and beyond" the normal scope of the teacher's job description. Finding ways to support stipends or extra pay is an important effort that the principal should consider. When warranted, the principal should ask, "How can I compensate and recognize the extra effort involved in this role?"

Fuel for Thought

- Plan for and schedule quarterly meetings for each teacher that lasts 20–40 minutes. Structure the meetings around their goals, and plan to ask the following questions: (1) How are your students doing? and (2) What can I do to support you? Listen to their responses. Then reflect and act. Teachers will come to expect this quarterly conversation and will keep their goals in mind.

- Remind your teachers that they are learners. In faculty meetings, take time to talk about the notion of adult learners, cognitive coaching, and the practical implications of each. Invite a district leader to (briefly) share a personal experience or show an online clip to jumpstart reflection and discussion. Make this relevant by connecting it to present challenges and successes within your school.

- Define teacher leadership roles. Many of these roles have been inherited from years past and do not have defined clarity. Consider how you might collaboratively align roles with current needs. Tweak them, if necessary, with teacher input. Offer incentives and support transparency in this work.

- Reflect on your current habits. What do you prioritize as you prepare for the school day? Consider what frustrates you most about routines in your present leadership role. What habits could help alleviate failure and enable greater success? How might your habits better support your teachers?

- Identify training and incentives. Think about what is needed to help ignite and grow your teacher leadership base. What training is needed to better equip your teachers to serve? How can you support your teachers in the important work they do? What affirmation, stipend pay, or professional time is available?

Creating a Culture of Collaboration

We must find ways to support what's working within our schools. However, a principal who spends most of his or her time behind an office desk will not have that proverbial finger on the pulse of the school. It's critically important to be an active, engaged (and engaging) leader immersed in the activity of the school, but visibility is not enough. We must provide feedback and affirmation and be a true part of the learning process. Again, the best principals never stop being teachers. It's in their blood. They roll up their sleeves, wear comfortable shoes, and aren't afraid to get down on the classroom floor, let loose on the dance floor, jump into a pick-up basketball game, or focus on what students are doing, learning, and saying. As a leader, it's important to remember that effective conversation is a two-way exercise.

Learn from Others

Antonetti and Garver (2015) note the incredible power of shifting the focus of walkthrough observations from what teachers are doing to what students are doing. For example, instead of immediately looking for a written objective on the classroom whiteboard, you might ask a student engaged in an activity, "Can you tell me what you are learning about and why this is relevant?" Reflecting on the work of our students can lead to powerful collaborations.

Alternatively, introduce and support the use of instructional rounds, which allows for shared discussion and reflection. Marzano (2011) emphasizes that rounds are not for evaluation but instead an opportunity for small groups of teachers to learn from one another. Consider stepping outside the school as well. As a high school principal, Baruti Kafele had the opportunity to take teams of educators to other schools to observe excellence, noting, "you cannot afford to lead in isolation" but instead learn and collaborate from those who have "already figured it out" (2015, p. 63). Principal support and encouragement can make this happen.

Support Teacher Goal Setting

Teacher evaluations often feel like an isolated practice rather than a collaborative opportunity. Even though states or districts may mandate a particular format, the principal should encourage, when feasible, one shared goal per team. This goal should be measurable and attainable within the scope of the school year, and it should be revisited in PLC meetings or during extended collaborative work time.

Examples of team goals might include (1) developing, administering, and adjusting formative assessments; (2) introducing new innovations and strategies to the rest of the team; and (3) collaboratively learning a second language using an online program to earn recertification points. A team goal serves to unify the team around a common, shared purpose while ensuring accountability.

Talk About the Vision

Think about how important your school's vision is to you as principal. Ask yourself, "Do my teachers and students also hold this vision dear?" Review your morning announcements, school (and principal) website, and your Twitter feed. Is your vision consistent and clear?

Be bold. In a faculty meeting, provide everyone with a slip of paper (or an anonymous online survey) where they can write about what they believe the school's vision to be. Read the answers aloud, and then take time to compare these responses to the school's official vision and mission statement. Chances are, the two are not aligned, and you have some work to do. Embrace this. Discuss, as a staff, what this means (or what it should mean). Be willing to facilitate meaningful conversations and change. Speak to the vision in your morning or afternoon announcements, highlight it in your daily e-mails, and celebrate real-life examples and successes.

As leaders, we are in a powerful position to help others grow, particularly if we have a shared vision of where we want to go and who we want to be. Connecting the vision to the work can serve as a catalyst for clarity, effort, and growth.

Take Something Off Teachers' Plates

A visionary leader with the best of intentions will still be a failure if he or she doesn't provide practical support to the successful, yet probably thoroughly overwhelmed, teacher. In this age of continuous change, teachers are understandably stressed. Principals should be aware of initiative fatigue and be proactive in taking something off teachers' plates. If we truly believe in the power of peer observations, for example, we shouldn't just issue a decree that they should happen; we should provide classroom coverage and a suggested schedule to align needs and resources.

Principal K. D. Umbarger at Mesa Elementary in Cortez, Colorado, is an example of a principal who still sees herself as a teacher. Like Principal Dingwall, she closely studied—and listened to—her teacher survey data. At Mesa, teachers indicated that they were overwhelmed with non-instructional duties such as hallway coverage and supervision. With that in mind, Principal Umbarger aligned resources—in her case, some extra funding—so she was able to hire parents as assistants who were responsible for monitoring interior school areas such as homework support areas, hallways, and transition areas. Believe me, her teachers took note.

"I wanted teachers to start their day on a positive note," recalled Umbarger (personal communication, 2015). She added, "We knew we had the students from 8 a.m. to 3 p.m. each day, and we wanted to maximize this time. I asked my staff to stop making excuses for what was outside their control and to choose action steps that we could control." One action step she took was to protect teacher time by adding this paid assistant time. This enabled teachers to devote more time to instruction and preparation, and subsequent survey data revealed that this key change was clearly appreciated by her teachers.

As principal, I knew the power of positive phone calls. Reaching out to parents in a proactive manner as a teacher—and then later as an administrator—was a powerful way of building positive capital with them. However, simply telling my teachers to follow my lead would just be another initiative. At the beginning of a faculty meeting, I spoke to the power of the positive phone call and gave them a few practical tips such as keeping a simple log (time, student and parent name, phone number, and brief bulleted summary) and being succinct and positive. I then told my teachers that this was so important to me that I was ending the faculty meeting right then and challenged them to go make a few calls. In other words, I showed that this was meaningful by respecting their time.

Fuel for Thought

- Prioritize visibility in the classroom and provide immediate feedback. Make walkthrough observations a daily practice. Be intentional to include specialists (non-core teachers) and vary the times of day you visit each classroom to get a truer sense of how teaching and learning occurs.
- Foster peer observations. Provide release time for in-depth, non-evaluative peer observations in which teachers can provide feedback to one another. Consider how you can help teachers see other classrooms (or schools) and implement changes in their own classrooms.
- Consider your school vision statement. Talk about it with your faculty. Reflect on this as a team. Seek your teachers' input and their support. Celebrate what is working.
- Share your vision statement. Review your website, daily (or weekly) communications with staff, newsletters or

messages home, and morning announcements. Do you weave the vision into your communication? Does it reflect the work—and the voice—of your teachers? Find ways to do this regularly.

- Take something off teachers' plates. If an initiative (such as one-on-one tutoring, updated hallway displays, or positive phone calls) is important to you as a leader, then consider something you might do to give your teachers the time to actually do it. End a meeting early, tweak the master schedule, or review current initiatives. Protect your teachers and streamline your school's work in a thoughtful manner.

Setting Goals as a Leader

Principals must set clear goals for themselves if they are to help teachers realize their own. Many have noted the power of writing daily goals to crystallize plans and to hold oneself accountable. Tom Frieden, director of the U.S. Centers for Disease Control, uses a half-folded index card to track his daily goals. He uses the outside of the card for his daily schedule and the inside to note "people I need to call and things I need to do"; he adds that "it keeps me on track and allows me to be proactive" (Alter, 2015, p. 93). Author Robert Morgan similarly advocates using a daily card to "devise a blueprint for the hours before you" (2015, p. 124).

As an educational leader, I have found immense benefit from writing my goals, working on them throughout my busy day, and reflecting on my progress at the end of the day. In education, we tend to favor acronyms, so here's one that should help busy principals begin to frame written goals and foster collaborative growth in the school: WATCH.

- **Welcome:** Consider how you ensure that all students, staff, and other stakeholders feel valued as a member of the learning community when they enter the school's learning spaces.
- **Affirm:** Find ways to celebrate the successes of both students and staff. Be specific and authentic, and connect these successes to the school's mission.
- **Teaching:** Spend time where learning happens. Be present. Engage. Ask questions to understand the perspective of both the learner and the teacher. Highlight actual strategies that are helping students learn.
- **Connect:** Consider how you will connect various aspects of the learning community together to help it grow stronger. Seek to match strengths with areas of need, and build learning communities outside of their usual silos.
- **Habit:** As you stay immersed in the literature and engaged in your PLN, identify one habit that will enable you to realize positive growth. (This book offers 30 such habits in the Fuel for Thought sections.) Write an action step that will help you leverage this strategy to realize success.

You might include on your daily card a few other "to do" items (e.g., those with pressing time lines or long-term goals) and an inspirational quote, poem, or verse you can share (see Figure 1). Your format will likely change over time, but it's important to find the right blend of "short-burst" actions and long-term visionary steps.

I've found that having a written list in hand makes a profound impact on what I'm able to accomplish and on how I reflect on my work and time. As the day progresses, I mark off what I've accomplished. It's refreshing to draw a line through a job well done. In brief moments peppered throughout the day, it's possible to reflect and reset while staying focused on key priorities.

Although I have relied on digital calendars and notes on my mobile device, I strongly recommend using an actual note card (paper!) as part of this habit. Physically reflecting on your daily goals, writing them down, and marking through completed tasks can help provide a tangible recognition of when you realize quick wins while simultaneously moving forward on long-term strategic goals.

FIGURE 1: **Daily Written Goals List**

Tuesday, September 8

Welcome: ~~After buses, visit all 7th grade pods for morning celebration announcement.~~

Affirm: Shout out to 6th grade science team on announcements for science fair; congratulate Ms. Garcia on completing her Master's degree. Plug the <u>vision</u> statement!

Teaching: Visit <u>all arts teachers</u> today, then 8th grade pod C; provide written feedback and reflective questions to each teacher immediately. Encourage dialogue!

Connect: Ask Ms. Jones if she can share the whiteboard drawing app during the next faculty meeting . . . connections with all science lab teachers? ~~Plan for Brad (elem principal) visiting tomorrow for monthly "Principal PLC" chat; let's visit math classrooms and look at student engagement.~~

Habit: Check in with office staff on scheduling quarterly meetings with all teachers; be sure teachers know format and that they have a chance to share highlights and concerns. <u>LISTEN, REFLECT, and ACT!</u>

"To Do":

~~Get quote on learning garden mulch.~~

Turn in budget draft to district office.

~~Check on status of recent language arts teacher hire.~~

Quote:

"Education is not the filling of a pail but the lighting of a fire."
William Butler Yeats

Fuel for Thought

- Begin each day with a time of quiet reflection, and create your own written list of daily goals on a note card. Consider the effect on teachers as you write your goals. Reflect on these goals at the beginning—and end—of each day and monitor your progress.

- Welcome members of the school community. Each day provides an opportunity for a new first impression as staff, students, and stakeholders arrive to school. How will they feel your presence? How will they interact with the school culture? Consider your entryways, lobby, office, and website. Are there artifacts of learning, community, and engagement that are evident?

- Affirm the accomplishments of students both inside and outside of the classroom. Look for unique contributions and achievements from faculty and staff as well. From a handwritten note to a verbal shout out on the morning announcements, your voice goes a long way in affirming this work!

- As principal, focus on teaching. Be a visible, engaged presence throughout the school. Focus on all subjects, from core (i.e., what's usually tested) to the arts (where teachers may feel more isolated), and look for ways to share effective strategies and practices. Ask your colleagues if they are willing to share a specific practice during a faculty meeting or PLC/department meeting. (Be specific about the format you expect.)

- Connect your teachers to what works. Remember, teachers do not typically have the same freedom and flexibility as principals to visit numerous classrooms. Keep an ear to the ground and consider how teachers can benefit from innovations and best practices. Provide insights and materials that are differentiated.

- Check in on your own leadership habits. What action steps will you take to ensure that those around you become better? Consider professional goals, your school improvement plan, and your school's mission and vision. Identify a habit that will enable you to realize your goals, and hold yourself accountable as you reflect on your work at the beginning and end of each day.

Connecting Others

The job of a principal grows difficult as demands increase and resources tighten. Add to the ever-changing role the realities of increasingly diverse learning communities, rapidly evolving innovations, and redefined notions of what "success" entails, and it's no wonder that the principalship is reaching a crisis point. In a 2014 report by the School Leaders Network, the authors noted the following: "Twenty-five thousand (one quarter of the country's principals) leave their schools each year, leaving millions of children's lives adversely affected.

Fifty percent of new principals quit during their third year in the role" (p. 1).

This stress and potential leadership turnover affects the students and staff in that school community in a profound manner. There are no quick fixes to this large-scale challenge, but much stands to be gained by embracing an ethos of collaborative leadership that is active and engaged in moving a school forward.

Collaboration happens when people are connected. Malcolm Gladwell defines connectors as "the kinds of people who know everyone" and who have relatively large social circles of acquaintances (2002, p. 38). By job description alone, principals are connectors. We come into contact with students, school faculty and staff, parents, community members, district staff, business and civic leaders, neighboring and feeder district community members, and—hopefully—an ever-growing online PLN. The question then becomes: How can we leverage our unique role as connectors to help others get fired up about leading?

Empower the Voice of the Teacher

As principals, we must continually seek to encourage our staff to learn—and contribute—in their roles as professional educators. Successful teachers must see themselves as producers—not just consumers—when it comes to the professional dialogue. Have you ever attended a conference or presentation about a dynamic strategy only to hear your own skeptical voice whisper, "Well, that wouldn't work in my school. This speaker wouldn't know how to handle my students"? It's time to turn this "my cynicism" into "we realism" by prioritizing the sharing and celebrating of hidden successes that are vibrant within our school walls.

Without key supports in place, though, a teacher's voice may be drowned out by the ever-growing classroom to-do list and roster of schoolwide priorities. Reeves (2008) notes that "the single greatest influence on the professional practices of teachers is the direct observation of other teachers" but adds that without systematic support in place, "great teachers remain islands of excellence, surrounded by oceans of well-intentioned teachers who lack the information, skills, and opportunities for practice that distinguish their most effective colleagues" (p. 70). Connecting great teachers with well-intentioned teachers is an important role that's squarely in the principal's court. Here are a few examples of how principals can work to empower the voice of their teachers.

Lead Effective Faculty Meetings

Often dreaded by teachers (and principals) as times of administrative minutiae, faculty meetings hold a powerful potential if principals prioritize the ABCs of affirmation, best practices, and coordinated collaboration (Sterrett, 2013). After reviewing feedback from teachers, Principal Eric Irizarry of D.C. Virgo Preparatory Academy, a public middle school in Wilmington, North Carolina, worked with a collaborative team to take this one step further. In seeking to transform faculty meetings into a time of sharing and collaboration, Eric invited his teachers to host the faculty meetings on a rotational basis in their classrooms.

After Eric opened the meeting and allowed time for affirmation, the host teacher would share a best practice. Regardless of the host teacher's subject of expertise, the "visiting" colleagues had a chance to experience teaching and learning in a new environment within their own building. The topics ranged from effective transitions to teaching strategies, but the focus was always on instruction. Conversations were teacher led and student focused . . . and teachers took notice. Instructional coach Sabrina Hill-Black notes, "it gives teachers an opportunity to see what goes on outside their classrooms and it invites teacher leadership opportunities" by encouraging professionals to share with and welcome their colleagues (personal communication, 2015).

Principals must emphasize both instructional and managerial aspects when it comes to leading, and what better way to grow teaching and learning than by letting the actual experts— the teachers themselves—weave together success stories of engaged students and effective lab rotations, for example. Principal Irizarry adds that "as the instructional leader, it's my responsibility to lead instructional initiatives in the school, but I don't have to deliver all the PD all the time. We found effective instructional strategies in the classroom, and I would ask that teacher to present in staff meetings" (personal communication, 2015). He adds that this built teacher leadership and strengthened overall capacity in the school.

Engage in School Improvement Planning

One key area in which principals must leverage the valuable work of teachers, students, and stakeholders is school improvement planning (SIP). Simply put, the principal's role is not that of a "lone ranger." Principals that act in isolation may find it difficult to maintain success in many aspects of their job, from school culture leadership to instructional leadership, which is why a shared approach is so critical.

One effective approach is the project management approach, wherein a teacher or other staff member (such as a counselor) is designated for each objective in the SIP. These project managers would oversee an objective and form a team of stakeholders who would "work out a day-to-day plan for tackling its objective" (Duke, Carr, & Sterrett, 2013, p. 36). Various teams would then form a larger committee—chaired by the principal or another staff member, such as a teacher— which would meet regularly to hear reports from the different teams on progress toward the objectives and to offer perspective and support.

This approach holds promise for realizing sustained success through shared ownership. Imagine if your school's SIP had three objectives—for example, an objective to increase student achievement in mathematics, one to bolster attendance, and another to enhance innovation in instruction— with a teacher at the helm of each objective. By having teachers lead efforts to realize success, the SIP process goes from an annual "sigh and trudge through it" checklist meeting to one in which teachers actually lead—and own—important components of the process. By being an involved, vibrant member of the larger SIP committee, the principal can help connect various objectives and stakeholders together in a meaningful way.

Support Teacher Innovation

As superintendent of Montezuma-Cortez Schools in Colorado, Alex Carter finds that one of the best things he can do as district leader is to listen to—and support—the teachers when it comes to decision making. By encouraging teachers and principals to think outside the box (or perhaps outside of the school), great ideas and innovations often emerge from within.

Just a short drive from Mesa Verde National Park, a vacant field on the grounds of a middle school provided an open green space for teachers and students to work with a local orchard to harvest heirloom fruit trees. Turning unused land into an engaging learning space helped students learn stewardship, science, and sustainability—and this work was made possible through Alex's support and his staff's willingness to think outside the school walls.

Principals must encourage their teachers to problem solve, innovate, and get out more. Teachers are often brimming with great ideas that some might consider unconventional. However, when leaders support healthy risk taking (and lead by example), there is literally no limit to what's possible.

Fuel for Thought

- Hold progressive faculty meetings. Don't fall into the habit of having all faculty meetings in the media center. Meet in learning spaces throughout the school, and start with a vibrant teacher-led discussion about student learning. Encourage host teachers to open meetings with short minilessons in their classrooms. Have fun and be practical; spend time considering transitions, student engagement, and formative assessment practices.

- Promote teacher ownership in your school improvement plan. Consider your SIP and reflect on the teachers' role. Are they owning this work? Have you empowered them to lead? What supports do they need? Consider next steps. How you will define and determine success?

- Showcase success. In your school office or lobby, maintain a running slideshow of pictures or a collection of artifacts from within the building that highlights positive examples of student learning, staff engagement, and volunteer contributions. Encourage teachers to send you pictures and work samples that align with the school's mission and vision.

- Consider practical support that would benefit your teachers. When you consider coverage of duties, paperwork items, and e-mail expectations, what supports could you provide as a leader that would help maximize the time and energy teachers spend on what matters most—instruction?

- Highlight teaching practices within the building as a part of every faculty meeting. Encourage and support time for teacher-led discussions. Ask yourself, "What would benefit me as a teacher?" Consider instructional strategies, innovations, learning spaces, and managerial aspects such as effective transitions.

Igniting Teacher Leadership Outside of School

So much of what we have shared so far involves what happens in and around the school. In this ever-expanding world of education, we must not limit teachers to boundaries drawn on a district map. As principals, we must support their work outside the school. We should consider ways to provide time and opportunities for teachers to learn and contribute as professionals. Here are a few examples.

Publish and Present

After years of university training, credentialing, and graduate school, the last thing many educators want to do is to write another paper. However, active, engaged practitioners have incredibly valuable insights and voices that must be heard. As principal, I realized the powerful potential of publishing and presenting on topics ranging from math exit slips to relationship building to innovations in the learning environment.

Teachers must be encouraged to share their ideas outside of school. I found it helpful, as principal, to lead the effort in crafting a manuscript or conference proposal and then asking teachers who were involved in the work to cowrite or copresent. This shared approach improved the final product immensely. Not only is it incredibly affirming for those presenting, but it also strengthens the profession to show real-time glimpses of successes and challenges present in today's schools.

Consider your ASCD state affiliate conference or other local, state, or regional gathering. Review guidelines and schedules. Encourage interactive (i.e., not "sit-and-get") sessions when presenting and really listen to feedback from the audience. Afterward, highlight these presentations in your school community and on your school website as you refine, revise, and prepare to present at a national or international conference!

Encourage Teacher Voice

One powerful way to encourage teacher voice is through the Edcamp model. Defined as "organic, participant-driven professional development experiences created by educators, for educators" where a variety of relevant discussions are collaboratively generated on the actual day of the event, these experiences are focused on a conversation delivery model as opposed to a typical presentation model (Edcamp Foundation, 2014, p. 7). Teachers guide these discussions, and principal support is key. Dr. Kristen Swanson, an Edcamp Foundation board member, notes that "the professional learning culture within a school is critical to the success of an Edcamp. Principals who support and value organic, participatory learning serve as models for their staff" (personal communication, 2015).

Edcamps require advance planning for logistics; learning spaces need to be secured, educators need to be invited and encouraged to participate, and discussion topics need to be generated. In keeping with adult learning theory, Edcamps are oriented around personalized professional goals. The day of the event begins with a blank schedule that is filled in by attendees. After a quick 15-minute kickoff delivered by the organizers to explain expectations, the sessions begin. The so-called rule of two feet (i.e., you can come and go according to interest and relevance) allows the groups to be both purposeful and meaningful (Edcamp Foundation, 2014).

Though this is a fantastic way for teachers to learn and share, Swanson emphasizes that the principal's role is important. She points out that it's essential for "principals who support Edcamps and organic learning to become Edcampers themselves. By being participants in organic learning, they are likely to increase excitement and momentum at their school sites" (personal communication, 2015). Principals can serve as an important source of encouragement by discussing—through the lens of adult learning—the importance of this sort of professional development while also finding ways, from a practical standpoint, to make this sort of learning experience possible.

Support External Professional Development Opportunities

Principals are ideally positioned to leverage external relationships—such as those with other schools, universities, or regional networks—as they help ignite and grow their teachers, who are often the most effective at leading these initiatives with supports in place. For example, in Roanoke, Virginia, elementary teacher Wade Whitehead has, since 2002, helped organize and lead the Teachers of Promise Institute, a two-day event that gathers the best and brightest prospective teachers from nearly three dozen college and university schools of education across the state. Whitehead explains that the institute celebrates the call to teach, elevates the teaching profession to the status it deserves, and activates its audience to galvanize world-class teaching and learning in public school classrooms.

After earning selection for the institute, each attendee is paired with a mentor (a practicing educator who has been recognized as a Milken National Educator, National Teacher of the Year, National Board Certified Teacher, or Regional or State Teacher of the Year). Mentors provide guidance and support to Teachers of Promise as they develop their professional skill sets, including development and presentation of practical workshops to equip the next generation of teachers for success in the ever-changing world of education. To date, more than 2,000 Teachers of Promise have been identified and recognized by Whitehead and his team.

In 2010, Whitehead established the Teachers of Promise Foundation, which funds the institute. A 501(c)(3) organization, the foundation is run by a board of directors from across the country and is anchored in Whitehead's classroom experience. His daily interactions with students and their families permit the foundation to respond, almost in real-time, to changes in instruction, curriculum, communication, and the actual experiences of classroom teachers. This agility and connectedness are unique assets that make the foundation's work nothing short of remarkable.

This sort of teacher-led effort requires an incredible time commitment and can be greatly strengthened by supporting administrators. "As a general rule, only great teachers can make great classrooms, and only great principals can make great schools," notes Wade Whitehead. "We must attract or develop—and then retain—high-caliber human capital if we are ever to navigate our true potential in schools. . . . Among other things, principals share one thing in common: They decided to take a career path that led them out of the classroom and up a tried-and-true career ladder. It is vitally important that principals come to understand and support classroom teachers who wish to lead while remaining in the classroom. This means that our principals and administrators have to challenge themselves to think differently about what advancement in the teaching profession can mean" (personal communication, 2015).

Important implications arise in terms of leadership roles, compensation, schedules, and professional development. If principals want to ignite and grow others—including teacher leaders who wish to stay in the classroom—they must be willing to make a commitment to allocate supporting resources.

Model an Engaged Online Presence

As a principal, I started using Twitter in 2009 to connect with other educators and thought leaders. From innovative superintendents to teacher leaders and university professors, I was exposed to innumerable topics related to my work. I realized that I also had much to share. Principals can learn and contribute to weekly Twitter chats, such as #atplc (Thursday nights), #satchat (Saturday mornings), and a variety of chats organized by topic or content area (e.g., #colchat - Culture of Learning Chat). By following—and participating in—conversations such as #edadmin (focused on school leadership) or #PBL (project-based learning), I have been able to enhance my own leadership perspective.

After learning about his work via Twitter, I visited Steven Weber while he was principal at Hillsborough Elementary School in Orange County Schools (North Carolina) and was amazed at the school's outdoor learning trails and amphitheater. The historic school also had personalized spaces and a learning commons area. Being able to learn about Weber's leadership via Twitter and then seeing him interact with his school community in person allowed me to see another example of leadership in action.

Weber notes, "Once you discover a network of educators, you will find that your growth points are endless" (personal communication, 2015). He adds that his PLN allows learning to be an "ongoing process of growing, evolving, and reflecting." This growing is critically important in moving the work of the school forward. Professional connections via social media can help us enhance our perspectives, make new connections, and learn about ideas outside our usual learning community in a powerful way.

Fuel for Thought

- Publish and present. As you read professional journals and books, and as you consider which conferences to attend, think about ways in which you and your teaching staff can share insights and successes. Map out dates and deadlines, and be willing to take a lead role in writing, securing funding, and encouraging others to step up!

- Foster Innovation. How might you support greater innovation in your school? Think about existing resources and support, and find ways to celebrate emerging technologies and strategies that are within your own walls.
- Encourage external development. You know it's important to get outside the school and connect with businesses, local houses of worship, and civic groups. Consider involving your teachers in this work. Seek their input and carve out time for them to connect with volunteers, share successes, and establish important relationships with external partners. Consider how they might contribute to a workshop or lead an Edcamp, and then initiate the necessary support.
- Affirm teacher leadership inside the classroom. Consider Wade Whitehead's model of leading as a classroom teacher. Think about ways to support leadership without pressuring excellent teachers into outside-the-classroom leadership roles. Many great teachers have chosen to remain in the classroom . . . to the benefit of many students. Empower and support them.
- Engage online. Lead by example by cultivating and maintaining an online presence. Showcase—in your daily e-mails, office lobby, or faculty meeting intros—a tip or insight gained during a Twitter chat, for example.

Modeling Healthy Habits

School leaders can fall prey to bad habits as well. When I'm busy, I am more prone to eating sodium-heavy fast food and quickly downing a soft drink packed with sugar and caffeine. If I'm mentally fatigued or emotionally drained, I may take a pass on exercising and channel surf instead. If this becomes a pattern, I know the toll it will take on my body. And when we're constantly looking out for our students and colleagues, our work can distract us from looking after our own well-being. It's difficult to focus on growing others if we're not keeping the right balance in our own lives. We must be an example at all times.

Consider how students and staff members spend much of their day at school. Chances are, most students—and more than a few teachers—spend a lot of time sitting down. Taking brief movement breaks can help refresh students mentally by providing a "reset" in the learning environment (Hallowell, 2012). Therefore, it's imperative that we encourage movement breaks in school. Identify examples where students are "learning loudly" through interactions and activity; don't simply look for an "ideal" of students seated quietly in rows when visiting classrooms. In addition, encourage your teachers to foster outdoor learning (Louv, 2012; Sterrett, 2013). Affirm, congratulate, and recognize teachers who resist the "sit-and-get" approach as the primary method of teaching.

It's hard to feel fired up if you're not healthy. Consider your own choices as an example. What are you eating for lunch at school? Are you active? Count your steps and your calories, and foster outside learning. Whenever possible, weave in practical advice and strategies, such as staying hydrated and providing healthy refreshments at meetings.

Fuel for Thought

- Count your steps. I often tell aspiring administrators, "Wear comfortable shoes!" The principal's role is not desk based. It is interactive and action oriented. Stay on the move and monitor your activity. A principal who is active within the learning community can proactively reduce being swamped in the office with issues. Challenge a principal colleague to see who is covering the most ground!
- Take learning outdoors. Educators play an important role in fostering a love of learning outside. Emphasize outdoor learning spaces, encourage teachers to maximize nature learning, and lead by example. Work with external partners to improve your grounds and make them more accessible for learning.
- Provide healthy snacks. When hosting a meeting, swap out the fried foods and sugary desserts for delicious healthy snacks and drinks.
- Stay hydrated. Ensure that students and staff have ample opportunity for water breaks. It's no joke that teachers don't have enough restroom breaks. Foster proper hydration by ensuring that water is readily available (and allowing coverage for breaks).

Time to Ignite Teacher Leadership

Remember the principal who helped us begin this journey? Pausing once more in front of the teachers' mailboxes in the late afternoon, she jotted a note to Ms. Jones, who had worked hard to implement a new whiteboard technology in her science classroom. "Thank you for taking the healthy risk to innovate," she wrote. "This would make a great lead in our next faculty meeting if you're willing to host." She placed the note in Ms. Jones's box, looked at her daily note card, marked off a daily goal, and looked once more at her daily quote from Yeats: "Education is not the filling of a pail but the lighting of a fire." She smiled, placed a check mark beside the quote, and put the card back into her pocket before heading home.

Today's teachers have an extraordinary number of options. The choice to teach the way they always have or innovate and learn from others in their PLN. The choice to remain a passive observer in faculty meetings and at conferences or become a powerful voice to the profession. The choice to let others do the heavy lifting required to move the school forward or play an active role in school improvement and visionary leadership. The choice to count down the days to retirement or make the most of every instructional moment both inside and outside the classroom.

The role of the principal is vital in capturing these moments and in realizing this growth. Now more than ever: it's time to ignite teacher leadership.

Acknowledgments

I am grateful for the voices of the educators in this book: Alex Carter, Budd Dingwall, Sabrina Hill-Black, Eric Irizarry, Kristen Swanson, K.D. Umbarger, Steven Weber, and Wade Whitehead. Thank you.

I would also like to thank the wonderful team at ASCD for their continued support for my contributions. Genny Ostertag, thank you for listening to ideas and for brainstorming with me. I also want to thank Jamie Greene for his thoughtful copy editing work.

To give your feedback on this publication and be entered into a drawing for a free ASCD Arias e-book, please visit
www.ascd.org/ariasfeedback

ascd | arias™

ENCORE

VIDEO TESTIMONIALS

These video testimonials expound on key themes from *Igniting Teacher Leadership.* Watch these short videos and discuss in a collaborative manner the related reflective questions and applications. What habits could help your school move forward in these areas? These brief insights from educators—who lead in the classroom, school, or district—serve to provide reflection on the importance of supporting teacher leadership in our schools.

Video #1: Retired principal Budd Dingwall speaks to the power of listening. Consider how you might "take the pulse" of your own school and foster regular check-ins with teachers. Link: http://youtu.be/f_ZxYLooj6M

Application: What do your teachers want to share with you? Consider what it would mean, logistically, to carve out 30–40 minute quarterly meetings with your teachers. How will this help realize your school's mission?

Video #2: Instructional coach Sabrina Hill-Black discusses the powerful potential of sharing best practices and fostering collaborative ownership with rotating faculty meetings. Link: https://youtu.be/5G1o0K_PvsY

Video #3: Principal Eric Irizarry adds that this built teacher leadership and capacity with the entire teaching staff. Link: https://youtu.be/sPnz5K0jcMo

Application: What do your "all-star" teachers have to share? Consider several teachers who could host the faculty meetings in their classrooms with a 15-minute introduction that could be focused on instruction, innovation, or effective transitions. Invite them and get their feedback or suggestions.

Video #4: Superintendent Alex Carter speaks to the importance of connecting a need with external partnerships in the local area to bolster student learning in a sustainable manner. Link: https://youtu.be/AsRNru52dXQ

Application: What are some ways you can maximize your learning spaces and involve local stakeholders? Conduct a grounds walk with teacher leaders at your school. Consider areas that could be improved as learning spaces. What supports are needed? How could you work to secure district resources and/or external funding to realize these goals?

Video #5: Teacher Wade Whitehead speaks to the importance of teacher leadership while being a teacher. Whitehead notes that administrators can make tremendous contributions to the notion of supporting and developing teacher leadership in the classroom. Link: https://youtu.be/INfnM7RI7jc

Application: How do you support teachers who choose to remain in the classroom? What implications does this have for professional development, leadership training, and funding supports?

Consider the educational leaders within your school and district. How can you support their voices and their perspectives? Think about ways you can celebrate success—from teaching strategies to collaborative innovations—and shine light on their respective voices. How can you ignite teacher leadership in your own school?

References

Alter, C. (2015 April 27). Power tools: The objects that inspire our influencers. *Time*, p. 93.

Antonetti, J. V., & Garver, J. R. (2015). *17,000 classroom visits can't be wrong: Strategies that engage students, promote active learning, and boost achievement.* Alexandria, VA: ASCD.

Bitterman, A., Goldring, R., & Gray, L. (2013). Characteristics of public and private elementary and secondary school principals in the United States: Results from the 2011–12 Schools and Staffing Survey. (NCES 2013-313). U.S. Department of Education. Washington, DC: National Center for Education Statistics. Retrieved from http://nces.ed.gov.pubsearch

Bond, N. (2015). Teacher leaders as professional developers. In N. Bond (Ed.). *The power of teacher leaders: Their roles, influence, and impact.* New York: Routledge.

Branch, G. F., Hanushek, E.A., & Rivkin, S. G. (2013). Measuring the impact of effective principals. *EducationNext, 13*(1), 62–69.

Costa, A. L., & Garmston, R. J. (2002). *Cognitive coaching: A foundation for renaissance schools (2nd ed.).* Norwood, MA: Christopher-Gordon.

Davis, B. H;, Gilles, C., McGlamery, S., Shillingstad, S. L., Cearley-Key, T., Wang, Y., Smith, J., & Stegall, J. (2015). Mentors as teacher leaders in school/university induction programs. In N. Bond (Ed.). (2015). *The power of teacher leaders: Their roles, influence, and impact.* New York: Routledge.

DeRosa, L. J., & Trostle Brand, S. (2015). Teacher leaders in curriculum reform: Integrating the expressive arts. In N. Bond (Ed.). *The power of teacher leaders: Their roles, influence, and impact.* New York: Routledge.

Duhigg, C. (2012). *The power of habit.* New York: Random House.

Duke, D. L., Carr, M., & Sterrett, W. (2013). T*he school improvement planning handbook: Getting focused for turnaround and transition.* Lanham, MD: Rowman & Littlefield.

Edcamp Foundation. (2014). *The Edcamp model: Powering up professional learning.* Thousand Oaks, CA: Corwin.

Gladwell, M. (2002). *The tipping point: How little things can make a big difference.* New York: Back Bay Books.

Gordon, G. (2013). School leadership linked to engagement and student achievement. Washington, DC: Gallup. Retrieved from http://www.gallup.com/services/176711/school-leadership-linked-engagement-student-achievement.aspx

Hallowell, E. (2012). Ferrari engines, bicycle brakes. *Educational Leadership, 70*(2), 36–38.

James, W. (1890). *Habit.* New York: Henry Holt and Co.

Kafele, B. K. (2015). *The principal 50: Critical leadership questions for inspiring schoolwide excellence.* Alexandria, VA: ASCD.

Louv, R. (2012). *The nature principle: Reconnecting with life in a virtual age.* Chapel Hill, NC: Algonquin.

Marzano, R. (2011). The art and science of teaching/Making the most of instructional rounds. *Educational Leadership, 68*(5), 80–82.

Morgan, R. (2015). *Mastering life before it's too late: Biblical strategies for a lifetime of purpose.* New York: Howard Books.

North Carolina's Teacher Working Conditions Initiative. (2012). 2012 results: Dr John Codington Elementary. Retrieved from http://2012.ncteachingconditions.org/reports

Reeves, D. (2008). *Reframing teacher leadership to improve your school.* Alexandria, VA: ASCD.

School Leaders Network. (2014). CHURN: The high cost of principal turnover. Retrieved from http://connectleadsucceed.org/sites/default/files/principal_turnover_cost.pdf

Smith, C. (2015). The special education teacher as a servant leader. In N. Bond (Ed.). *The power of teacher leaders: Their roles, influence, and impact.* New York: Routledge.

Sterrett, W. (2011). I*nsights into action: Successful school leaders share what works.* Alexandria, VA: ASCD.

Sterrett, W. (2013). *Short on time: How do I make time to lead and learn as a principal?* Alexandria, VA: ASCD.

Sterrett, W. (2015). Maximizing teacher leadership: The principal as facilitator. In N. Bond, Ed. *The power of teacher leaders: Their roles, influence, and impact.* New York: Routledge.

Teacher Leadership Exploratory Consortium (2011). The teacher leader model standards. Retrieved from www.ets.org/s/education_topics/teaching_quality/pdf/teacher_leader_model_standards.pdf

Welch. J., with Welch, S. (2005). *Winning.* New York: HarperCollins.

York-Barr, J., & Duke, K. (2004). What do we know about teacher leadership? Findings from two decades of scholarship. *Review of Educational Research, 74*(3), 255–316.

Related Resources

At the time of publication, the following ASCD resources were available (ASCD stock numbers appear in parentheses). For up-to-date information about ASCD resources, go to www.ascd.org. You can search the complete archives of *Educational Leadership* at http://www.ascd.org/el.

ASCD EDge®

Exchange ideas and connect with other educators on the social networking site ASCD EDge® at http://ascdedge.ascd.org.

Print Products

100+ Ways to Recognize and Reward Your School Staff by Emily E. Houck (#112051)

Insights Into Action: Successful School Leaders Share What Works by William Sterrett (#112009)

Learning From Lincoln: Leadership Practices for School Success by Harvey Alvy & Pam Robbins (#110036)

Retaining New Teachers: How do I support and develop novice teachers? by Bryan Harris (#SF115054)

School Climate Change: How do I build a positive environment for learning? (ASCD Arias) by Peter DeWitt & Sean Slade (#SF114084)

School Leadership That Works: From Research to Results by Robert J. Marzano, Timothy Waters, & Brian A. McNulty (#105125)

Short on Time: How do I make time to lead and learn as a principal? by William Sterrett (#SF114044)

The Tech-Savvy Administrator: How do I use technology to be a better school leader? by Steven W. Anderson (#SF115015)

For more information: send e-mail to member@ascd.org; call 1-800-933-2723 or 703-578-9600, press 2; send a fax to 703-575-5400; or write to Information Services, ASCD, 1703 N. Beauregard St., Alexandria, VA 22311-1714 USA.

About the Author

 William Sterrett serves as an associate professor and program coordinator at the University of North Carolina, Wilmington. Previously, as a principal in Virginia, Sterrett received the 2008 Milken National Educator Award. Sterrett earned his B.S. in Middle Grades Education from Asbury College (Kentucky) and his Ph.D. in Educational Administration & Supervision from the University of Virginia, and he is the author of the ASCD books *Insights Into Action: Successful School Leaders Share What Works* and *Short on Time: How do I make time to lead and learn as a principal?* Sterrett can be reached at sterrettw@uncw.edu and followed on Twitter at @billsterrett.

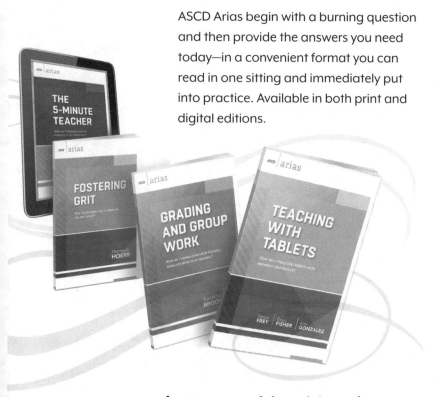